D0230076

90710 000 313 461

GO FACTS SPACE

The Solar System

A & C BLACK • LONDON

The Solar System

contents

© Blake Publishing 2006
Additional material © A & C Black Publishers Ltd 2006

First published in Australia in 2006 by Blake Education Pty Ltd

This edition published in the United Kingdom in 2006 by
A & C Black Publishers Ltd, 38 Soho Square, London W1D 3HB
www.acblack.com

Hardback edition
ISBN-10: 0-7136-8386-4
ISBN-13: 978-0-7136-8386-8

Paperback edition
ISBN-10: 0-7136-8384-8
ISBN-13: 978-0-7136-8384-4

A CIP record for this book is available from the British Library.

Written by Maureen O'Keefe
Publisher: Katy Pike
Editor: Paul O'Beirne
Design and layout by The Modern Art Production Group

Photo credits: Title Page, p14 (b), p15 (tr), p19 (tl) pictures courtesy NASA; p5 (tl,
bl) (photolibrary.com); p4 (bl), p17 (tl), p21 (tr, bl), p23 (tr, br), p25 (bl) (australian
picture library); pp28–29 (Paul McEvoy). Illustrations on pp6–7: Toby Quarmby.
Illustration on p24: Luke Jurevicius.

Printed in China by WKT Company Ltd.

Our Solar System

The solar system is the Sun and all the different objects that orbit around it. These objects include the eight classical planets, their moons and asteroids and comets.

Circling the Sun

The Sun is a star, which means it is a huge, spinning ball of hot gas. It is the only star in our solar system and it provides light and heat to the planets. The Sun's **gravity** is the force that holds the solar system in place and keeps the planets travelling around the Sun.

The planets

Mercury, Venus, Earth and Mars are the four planets closest to the Sun. They are rocky planets with a metal **core**. The next four planets, Jupiter, Saturn, Uranus and Neptune, are gas planets. They have rocky cores covered by liquid or ice, with layers of gas clouds on the outside. As well as these classical planets, there are smaller planets called dwarf planets.

Moons are large, rocky **satellites** that **orbit** a planet. Each classical planet has at least one moon, except for Mercury and Venus which don't have any.

Asteroids are pieces of rock that orbit the Sun. Most asteroids are grouped together in a 'belt' between Mars and Jupiter. Comets are made of ice, dust and rock.

4

The inner solar system is separated from the outer by the asteroid belt.

Asteroid belt

The dwarf planet Pluto was considered equal in status with the classical planet until August 2006, when the word 'planet' was redefined to exclude any bodies which overlap the orbit of another. Pluto's orbit crosses the path of Neptune.

Our solar system

The solar system is part of the Milky Way galaxy, which is a barred-spiral galaxy.

GO FACT!

DID YOU KNOW?

If all the planets were joined together, the Sun would still be more than 700 times bigger. It contains over 99% of the solar system's **mass**.

Model of the Solar System

Sun

Mercury

Venus

Earth

Moon

Mars

Phobos

Deimos

Ganyme

Asteroid Belt

Neptune

Comet

Triton Nereid

Titania

Ariel

Saturn

Oberon

Uranus

Miranda Puck

Enceladus

Rhea
Tethys

Umbriel

Mimas

Lepetus

Phoebe

Jupiter

Dione Titan Hyperion

Europa Callisto

Io

Interstellar dust

Asteroids

Asteroid

7

The Sun

The Sun is only an average-sized star, but the energy it produces allows life to exist on Earth.

Solar energy

The Sun is a yellow **dwarf star**. Like all stars, it is a huge ball of spinning gas. Energy is produced in the Sun's core and travels to the outer part of the Sun. The high temperature and intense pressure create powerful **nuclear reactions** within the Sun's core. Atoms of hydrogen smash together and fuse to form helium. This produces light and heat energy. The energy **radiates** outwards to the surface of the Sun, which is called the photosphere.

The speed of light

From the Sun's surface, light and other **radiation** travel to other parts of the solar system, including Earth. It takes 8 minutes and 17 seconds for this energy to reach Earth, which is 150 million kilometres (93 million miles) away from the Sun.

The Sun's energy is essential for life on Earth. It provides light for plants to grow – the basis of all food chains. The Sun also provides heat, which creates our weather. The water cycle depends on this heat to bring about water evaporation – this forms clouds and rain.

It takes two million years for **gamma rays** produced in the core of the Sun to reach its surface.

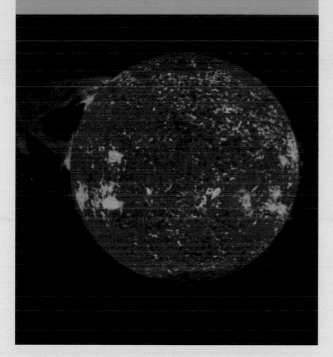

The Sun is the largest object in the solar system. It is about 332 950 times more massive than Earth.

The relationship between the Sun and the Earth drives the seasons, currents in the ocean, weather and climate.

GO FACT!

DID YOU KNOW?

The Sun has been burning for about five billion years and will burn for another five billion.

9

Mercury and Venus

Mercury and Venus are the two planets closest to the Sun. The conditions on each planet are very different.

Rocky planets

Both Mercury and Venus are made of solid rock, but they look completely different. About 60% of Mercury's surface is covered in **craters**, caused by **meteorites** crashing into the planet. This makes it look very similar to Earth's moon. Venus has many volcanoes.

There is a major difference between the **atmospheres** on the two planets. Mercury has almost no atmosphere. Venus has a thick atmosphere of carbon dioxide, covered by spinning clouds of **sulphuric acid**.

Temperature

Although Mercury is the closest planet to the Sun, Venus is actually the hotter planet. Mercury's temperature reaches 427°C during the day. Since there is no atmosphere to trap heat near the surface of the planet, the temperature falls to −180°C at night. On Venus, any heat that finds its way through the thick atmosphere is trapped near the surface of the planet, producing a **greenhouse effect**. The temperature reaches 480°C. This heat also means water cannot exist as a liquid on either Mercury or Venus.

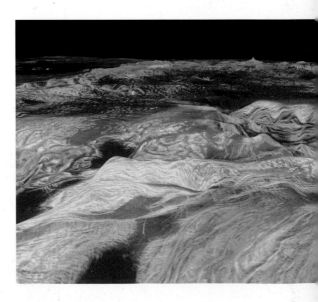

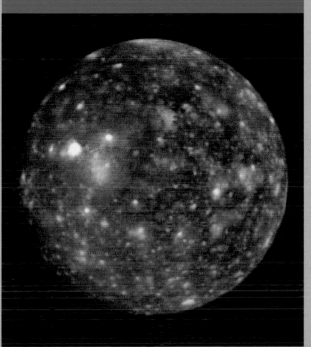

If you stood on Venus, the atmospheric pressure would be the same as if you were 900 metres underneath an ocean on Earth.

Much of the surface of Venus, including craters, has been covered in lava from previous eruptions.

Mercury and Venus are the only two planets in our solar system that don't have moons.

GO FACT!

GREATEST VARIATION

Mercury has the greatest variation in surface temperature of any planet in the solar system – over 600°C.

Earth and Its Moon

Earth is unique amongst the planets in our solar system. It is the only one with all the conditions needed for life to exist.

Earth is the only planet with a temperature that allows liquid water to exist. The other planets are either too close to the Sun, or too far away. It is also the only planet to have an atmosphere that contains 21% oxygen, which we need to breathe, and 78% nitrogen. This atmosphere protects Earth from the Sun's **ultraviolet** rays. It also traps some of the Sun's heat and transports liquid around the planet in the form of rain.

Earth only has one satellite – the Moon. It is about a quarter of the size of Earth and has no water, wind, air or atmosphere. The Moon is held in orbit by Earth's gravity. On Earth, we only ever see the same side of the Moon. This is because the Moon takes the same time to spin on its **axis** as it does to orbit the Earth. Although the Moon only has weak gravity, it is close enough to Earth to affect our oceans. It is the Moon that causes the rise and fall of our tides.

Because there is no wind or rain on the Moon, any footprints left by the astronauts should remain for millions of years.

It is thought that Earth was once hit by a large object, and the debris that was ejected into space joined together to form the Moon.

The official Latin name for planet Earth is Terra. It is named after the Roman goddess of fertility and growth, Terra Mater.

GO FACT!

DID YOU KNOW?

The Moon is the only other planet or satellite in the solar system that humans have set foot upon.

13

Mars

Mars is a red planet with some similar features to Earth. It is still not known whether Mars has ever supported life.

Similar features

The soil on Mars contains iron oxide, which gives the planet its red colour. Iron oxide is a mineral also found in Earth's soil.

There is evidence that water once flowed on the Martian surface. There are valleys, that have been eroded by water, and dry riverbeds. Mars has icecaps at its north and south poles, like Earth.

The length of a Martian day is about 40 minutes longer than a day on Earth. Mars also has a similar tilt on its axis to Earth, so it has the same pattern of seasons.

Volcanoes occur on Mars. In fact, Olympus Mons is the largest volcano in the solar system. It is 25 kilometres (15.5 miles) high and 600 kilometres (373 miles) wide.

Cold with no oxygen

There are significant differences between the atmospheres on Mars and on Earth. Mars has a very thin atmosphere of carbon dioxide, which means that we could not survive on Mars.

Mars is a very cold planet. The temperature falls to as low as −120°C with a maximum of around 0°C. Winds on Mars can cause huge dust storms, which cover the whole planet.

The length of each Martian season is almost twice as long as a season on Earth.

Mars has the least hostile environment of all the other planets in the solar system.

The surface area of Mars is approximately equal to that of Earth's dry land. Mars does not have any oceans.

GO FACT!

DID YOU KNOW?

Mars has two small moons. They have uneven shapes and may originally have been asteroids.

15

Jupiter and Saturn

Jupiter is the largest planet in the solar system and has the fastest rotation. Saturn is the second-largest planet, surrounded by rings of ice-covered rock. Both are gas giants.

Jupiter

If all the other planets were combined into one, its mass would be less than half of Jupiter's. It is 1300 times larger than Earth.

Jupiter completes its **rotation** in less than ten hours. This speed results in strong winds and huge cloud bands. Strong storms develop when these bands of clouds meet. One hurricane, known as the Great Red Spot, has existed for over 300 years.

Saturn

Like Jupiter, Saturn is made of hydrogen and helium gas. Saturn's rotation is almost as fast as Jupiter's. Saturn also has very strong winds, reaching speeds that are 11 times faster than a hurricane on Earth.

There are thousands of rings surrounding Saturn. Each ring contains pieces of ice and rock travelling in orbit around Saturn. The rings closer to the planet seem to hold larger pieces, while the outer rings contain finer materials.

Both Jupiter and Saturn have many satellites, some discovered only very recently. Jupiter seems to have the most moons of any planet in our solar system – at least 62. Saturn has more than 30.

After the Sun, the Moon and Venus, Jupiter is usually the fourth brightest object in the sky.

Saturn is almost exactly the same as Jupiter, just smaller. The only striking difference is the rings around Saturn.

GO FACT!

DID YOU KNOW?

Jupiter is made of hydrogen and helium gases, which also make up the Sun. If Jupiter had been bigger, it could have become a star.

Saturn's rings are thought to be particles of an old moon, which was smashed to pieces in a collision, million of years ago.

Uranus, Neptune and Dwarf Planets

The two furthest planets from the Sun are Uranus and Neptune. They are both gas planets with a blue-green appearance. There are also some dwarf planets in our solar system.

Blue-green methane

Both Uranus and Neptune have atmospheres of hydrogen, helium and methane. The methane gives these planets a blue-green colour. Below the atmosphere, both planets have liquid layers of **water ice**, methane and ammonia around small, rocky cores.

Uranus

Uranus, its rings and moons all orbit the Sun, tipped on their side (see pages 6–7). This may have been caused by a collision with another huge object. The result is that each pole on Uranus receives 42 Earth years of sunlight, followed by 42 years of darkness.

Neptune

Neptune, like Uranus, has rings and moons. It has a stormy atmosphere and has the fastest recorded winds in the solar system. These storms may be caused by heat generated within Neptune.

Dwarf planets

Pluto was downgraded in status from a classical planet to a dwarf planet in August 2006. There are a number of other dwarf planets in our solar system, including Ceres, which sits between Mars and Jupiter, and UB313.

It takes 84 Earth years for Uranus to complete one full orbit around the Sun.

Some scientists think that Pluto is an icy asteroid from the **Kuiper Belt**.

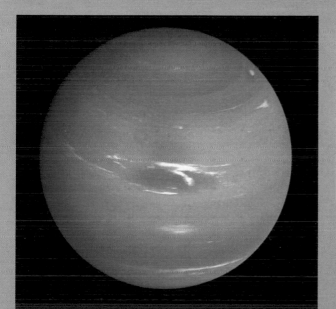

As its orbit is so far from the sun, Neptune receives very little heat — in fact the uppermost regions of its atmosphere are –218°C.

GO FACT!

DID YOU KNOW?

Pluto is not the first planet to be downgraded in status. Ceres was considered a planet when it was discovered in 1801.

Asteroids, Meteoroids and Comets

Asteroids are pieces of rock and iron that orbit the Sun. Meteoroids are smaller bits of material that fly through space. Comets orbit the Sun, and are made of ice, dust and rock.

Asteroids

Asteroids are sometimes known as 'minor planets' although they can range in size from a few metres across to almost 1000 km (621 miles) wide. Many asteroids are found orbiting in an asteroid belt between Mars and Jupiter.

Meteoroids

Meteoroids travel at great speed. When they enter Earth's atmosphere, they burn up due to friction with the air. These streaks of light are called meteors, or shooting stars. If meteors don't burn up completely, due to their large size, they hit Earth's surface. These are called meteorites. The Barrington Crater in Arizona, USA, was formed when a 30–50 metre iron meteorite hit Earth about 50 000 years ago. It is one of about 120 impact craters on Earth.

Comets

There are billions of comets orbiting the Sun. A comet doesn't have a tail for most of its orbit. As a comet moves closer to the Sun, it begins to warm up. Gas and dust from the nucleus, or solid icy centre of the comet, begin to form a cloud or a 'coma' around the nucleus. The Sun and its solar wind blow the coma into two tails, one of gas and one of dust. As the comet moves away from the Sun, the tails shrink.

Halley's comet is the best known periodic comet with the first recorded sighting being in China in 240 BC. It returns to Earth every 75–76 years. Its next visit to the inner solar system will be the summer of 2061.

A comet's tail can be millions of kilometres long.

Over 9000 asteroids have been located and named.

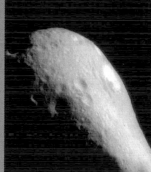

GO FACT!

DID YOU KNOW?
Halley's comet last visited Earth in 1986.

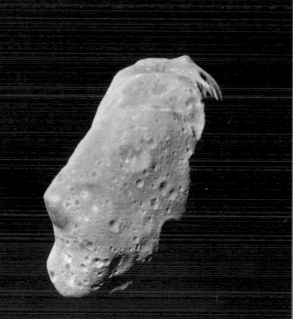

An asteroid, called Ida, has its own moon (called Dactyl).

Are NEOs a Threat to Earth?

Near-Earth-Objects (NEOs) are small objects in the solar system. They have struck Earth in the past and will definitely hit again, but are we in danger?

The Earth has been hit by asteroids, comets and meteorites in the past. Scientists believe that when a large asteroid collided with Central America 65 million years ago the dinosaurs became extinct. The collision threw up water and rock which hid the Sun and covered the Earth in darkness for months. Dinosaurs could not survive in the cooler climate.

Most meteors are tiny and burn up in Earth's atmosphere. Even the ones that do get through and land as meteorites are mostly very small. The Earth's atmosphere protects us from all objects up to about 40 metres across.

Asteroids pose a much bigger threat to Earth as they tend to be much larger objects. If an asteroid with a diameter of more than two kilometres hit the Earth, it would cause a catastrophic planetary event. Many people would die as a result of the impact and of the Earth entering a long cold winter where most crops would die. The good news is that an asteroid of this size only collides with Earth about once every 100 million years.

The Spaceguard survey scans the skies looking for any dangerous NEOs. As yet, none that are on a collision course with Earth have been discovered. When a bigger object does head our way, we should have the advance warning and technology to deal with it.

Astronomers look in space for asteroids or meteorites that might be headed towards Earth.

When small fragments of cosmic debris, often left over from a passing comet, enter Earth's atmosphere at high speed we get a meteor shower.

Today, in the United States and Australia, we can still see craters that are the result of meteorites hitting Earth.

Huge asteroids, like the one that caused the extinction of the dinosaurs, collide with Earth about once every 100 million years. That asteroid was 15 km (9.3 miles) wide.

Seasons on Earth

Earth's **revolution** around the Sun creates the seasons. They are different in the Northern and Southern Hemispheres.

Why do we have seasons?

Earth completes a revolution around the Sun every $365\frac{1}{4}$ days. It is this orbit, combined with the tilt on Earth's axis, which causes the seasons. The tilt of approximately 23.5 degrees, means that the Earth leans slightly towards the Sun.

For part of the year, the Northern **Hemisphere** is tilted towards the Sun. During this time, the Sun is closer to the Northern Hemisphere. This means the Northern Hemisphere is in the direct path of the Sun's energy. As the Sun's rays hit Earth, they are concentrated, because they've travelled less distance through the atmosphere. The Sun rises higher in the sky, and produces longer days. This is the Northern Hemisphere's summer.

At the same time, the Southern Hemisphere is tilted away from the Sun. The Sun's rays hit Earth at an angle. The Sun's energy is weaker as it has travelled through more of the atmosphere. The Sun doesn't rise as high in the sky, and the days are shorter. This is winter in the Southern Hemisphere.

When it is summer in the Southern Hemisphere, it is winter in the Northern Hemisphere and vice versa.

In some regions of the planet, like India, people refer to wet and dry seasons instead of the four seasons.

DID YOU KNOW?

When it is spring and autumn, neither hemisphere is tilted toward the Sun.

Day and Night

Earth's rotation on its axis causes day and night.

As Earth spins, sunlight only falls on one-half of the planet. This means it is daytime on that side of Earth. On the other side, it is night.

The apparent movement of the Sun across the sky is actually due to the rotation of our Earth. The Sun always appears to rise in the east, and set in the west, regardless of where you are on Earth.

When the Sun rises, that part of the Earth is turning to face the Sun. When the Sun sets, that part of the Earth is turning away from the Sun. The Sun itself doesn't actually 'rise' or 'set'.

Each planet spins around, or rotates, on its axis at a speed of 1600 km/h (994 mph). Earth takes almost 24 hours to complete one rotation around the Sun. Because each rotation takes slightly less than 24 hours the calendar needed adjusting. Leap years add an extra day, the 29th February, to the calendar every four years so that the calendar aligns with Earth's motion around the Sun.

Moon phases

We see the Moon because sunlight is reflected from its surface. As the Moon orbits Earth, and as Earth orbits the Sun, we see different amounts of the Moon's sunlit face. These are known as the phases of the Moon.

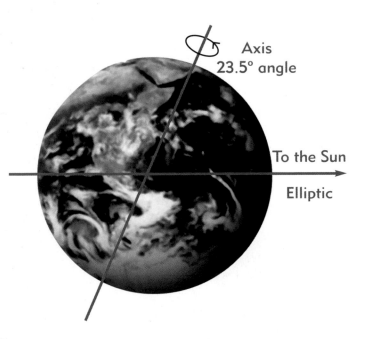

Axis
23.5° angle

To the Sun

Elliptic

Phases of the Moon

Waxing Gibbous
More than one-half of the Moon is lit by direct sunlight.

Full Moon
Two weeks after the New Moon, the Moon is halfway through its orbit. The Moon's sunlit side is facing Earth.

First Quarter
One-half of the Moon is lit by direct sunlight.

Waning Gibbous
More than one-half of the Moon is lit by direct sunlight.

Waxing Crescent
Less than one-half of the Moon is lit by direct sunlight.

Last Quarter
One-half of the Moon is lit by direct sunlight.

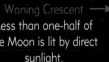

New Moon
The Moon is between Earth and the Sun, and the Moon's unlit side is facing Earth.

Waning Crescent
Less than one-half of the Moon is lit by direct sunlight.

Phases of the Moon

Nights on average are shorter than days. This is because even when then Sun has gone down, its light still reaches the ground, because of the way it passes through the atmosphere.

The Moon's surface doesn't give off any light, it reflects the light of the Sun.

27

Solar Eclipse

Sometimes the Moon moves between the Sun and the Earth so the three are in a straight line. The Moon blocks the Sun's light, and part of the Earth is in the Moon's shadow. This is a solar eclipse.

Discover what happens in a solar eclipse.

What you need:

- globe of the Earth
- ball with string attached (Moon)
- torch (Sun)

1 Place the Earth, Moon and Sun in line so that the Moon is in the middle.

3 Rotate the Earth so that the eclipse occurs where you live.

2 Turn on the Sun and observe the shadow that falls on a small part of Earth.

Table

Planet	Size (compared to Earth)	Interesting Fact
Sun	332 950 x Earths	The Sun is so massive its interior could hold 1.3 million Earths.
Mercury	0.055 x Earths	Because of its **proximity** to the Sun the average surface temperature on Mercury is 179°C.
Venus	0.815 x Earths	Venus was named after the Roman goddess of love and beauty. This is probably due to the fact Venus is very bright in the night sky in comparison to the other planets.
Earth	1 x Earth	The Earth's surface is comprised of 71% water. Earth is the only planet that has liquid water on its surface.
Mars	0.107 x Earths	The solar day on Mars is very close to Earth's: 24 hours, 39 minutes and 35.244 seconds.
Jupiter	317.8 x Earths	Although Jupiter consists mainly of gas, its core is quite different. It consists of rocky material which equals roughly the mass of 10–15 Earths.
Saturn	95.162 x Earths	Because Saturn's core is so hot it radiates more energy into space than it receives from the Sun.
Uranus	14.536 x Earths	Uranus, like Saturn, Jupiter and Neptune, also has rings. All the rings are very faint. The outermost ring, known as the Epsilon, is comprised mostly of ice boulders, several feet across.
Neptune	17.147 x Earths	Neptune has the strongest winds recorded of any planet. They can reach up to 2000 km/h (1243 mph).

Glossary

atmosphere layer of gases surrounding a planet

axis an imaginary line which passes through a planet, from the North to the South Pole

core the central part of a planet

crater a hollow resulting from the collision of an object with a planet

dwarf star a smaller-sized star (our Sun is a yellow dwarf star)

elliptical the shape of an oval

gamma rays high-energy waves that come from a radioactive source

gravity the force that attracts all bodies in the Universe to each other

greenhouse effect the heating that occurs when gases trap heat and stop it from escaping a planet's atmosphere

hemisphere one half of a planet

Kuiper Belt disk-shaped region of minor planets and ice outside the orbit of Neptune

mass the amount of matter in an object

meteorite piece of metal or stone from outer space that has reached Earth

nuclear reaction collision of atoms giving off energy

orbit the path that an object makes, around another object

proximity closeness between two objects

radiates giving off heat or light

radiation the release of energy in the form of waves or rays

revolution the movement of a heavenly body in an orbit around another heavenly body

rotation turning round and round, like a wheel

satellite an object that revolves around a planet

sulphuric acid a strong mineral acid

ultraviolet invisible rays in sunlight

waning getting smaller

water ice water frozen in the solid state

waxing getting bigger

Index